Bestselling, Awa

CHRIS & KARENE LAMBERT-(

THE

YEAR THE

WORLD

CHANGED

HOW TO SURVIVE AND THRIVE
IN UNCERTAIN TIMES

In collaboration with
ALICE COOKE, ANNA GOODWIN, AMY ROGERS, DAVID ROYLANCE,
JANE MCDOWELL, SARAH HAMON WATT, SHARON BETTERTON

The Legal Bit

Limits of Liability and Disclaimer of Warranty

The author and publisher shall not be liable for your misuse of the enclosed material. This book is strictly for informational and educational purposes only.

Warning - Disclaimer

The purpose of this book is to educate and entertain. The author and/or publisher do not guarantee that anyone following these techniques, suggestions, tips, ideas, or strategies will become successful. The author and/or publisher shall have neither liability nor responsibility to anyone with respect to any loss or damage caused, or alleged to be caused, directly or indirectly by the information contained in this book.

Medical Disclaimer

The medical or health information in this book is provided as an information resource only and is not to be used or relied on for any diagnostic or treatment purposes. This information is not intended to be patient education, does not create any patient-physician relationship, and should not be used as a substitute for professional diagnosis and treatment.

HCB Publishing Ltd.
London | United Kingdom
Printed in EU, UK, Canada and the United States of America

ISBN: 978-1-8380061-1-2

DEDICATION

To Our Team at Heart Centred Business,
You make this company the success that it is, thank you!

To Our Clients,
You inspire us to do better, always!

To everyone impacted by the Covid Pandemic,
You're not alone.
Stay true to your values, keep moving forward
and we can change this world together!

Chris and Karene Lambert-Gorwyn are on a mission to create 1000 heart-centred millionaires.

Why millionaires?

Because whether we like it or not, most problems in life can be made better if you have more money. Money gives us choices; it opens up possibilities and provides access to more resources and solutions. Whilst many people react against and resist this notion, the reality is that not having enough money is one of the biggest causes of stress and challenges in life. What if you could change that?

Imagine if you had more money...

What changes would you make in your life?

What would now be possible for your family, your community, your charitable projects?

What difference could you make in the world if you had more money?

This is the mission Chris and Karene are on.

Would you like to join them?
+44 (0)333 987 4245
hello@heartcentredbusiness.com

THE BACKGROUND...

Chris and Karene created Heart Centred Business in 2015: a unique company helping business owners to grow themselves and their businesses from passion to profit. Typically, their clients earn an extra £50,000 – £100,000 within 12 months of implementing their systems.

Having built multiple 5, 6 and 7-figure businesses themselves, written numerous #1 best-selling books and created a nationwide property portfolio, Chris and Karene have developed a system for creating outstanding business results regardless of what is happening in the world. It is this system that they teach their clients and, to date, they have changed the businesses – and lives – of more than 3,000 clients.

Chris and Karene's system can be broken down into three steps:

Knowledge and Strategy: Do the right things in the right order. Know WHAT to do, HOW to do it and, most importantly, WHEN to do it.

Mindset: Your biggest obstacle is always YOU.
Clearing your internal blocks and self-sabotage patterns is the only way to achieve absolutely anything you want.

Community: Pick your people wisely as they will either make or break your success.
Surrounding yourself with like-minded people, who share your values and will support your growth and success.

In this book, Chris and Karene have brought together their core team of employees from Heart Centred Business to share the key lessons they have learned or had to apply both as individuals and as a company, as a result of the global coronavirus pandemic. This book contains business tips, strategies and personal stories gleaned from their collective experiences, all with the aim of changing the way you think about life and business in order to move you forward NO MATTER WHAT HAPPENS AROUND YOU.

Chris and Karene want you to learn from both their successes and their failures, as well as those of their team. This applies to business, but also to your own personal development because a business can only develop to the level of growth of the person running the business. It is this integration of personal and business growth that creates a heart centred business and is one of the reasons their clients get such great results.

Life keeps happening and dramas will always occur. The only thing you can control is how you respond. This book is designed to give you some tools and different ways of responding so no matter what life throws at you, whether it's local, national or global, you have the ability, the mindset and the resources to keep moving forward.

The three main themes of the book

1. Mindset: Keeping an open mind and finding a way.

2. Decisions lead to action: Every decision is important, no matter how small because decisions move you forward, indecision keeps you stuck.

3. Persistence: Find a system that works for you, then stick to it long enough to get results.

Individually, the Heart Centred Business Team who feature in this book, are 10 very different people, with 10 different backgrounds, personalities and experiences, united by our passion for making a difference in the world and teaching people how to be self-reliant and resourceful. We know this sounds cliché but it's true and it's what makes us a team.

We have shared experiences of success, joy, struggle, of varying degrees of adversity and failure, of challenges and obstacles that we have had to overcome in order to thrive. And in the sharing and learning from this shared experience we call life, we support each other to grow so we can overcome bigger obstacles and tackle greater challenges. Because it is our belief that success is the growth that comes from these experiences and is what being alive is about. If we look at the natural world, if you aren't growing, you are dying and whilst this is an inevitability for us all, let's make sure that the time we have is the best it can be.

The coronavirus pandemic was another example of a shared life experience that challenged us individually in very different ways. As a period of massive upheaval, uncertainty, pain and fear experienced by the entire world, it really highlighted that we are all in it together. But everyone's individual experience was different and whilst some people and businesses were broken by the pandemic, others have shined.

We don't promise to have all the answers. We definitely don't think our way of doing things is the only way. We, like you, are always looking to learn more and grow so we can show up in this world even better. However, individually, and as a team, we do have some suggestions and learning that might help move you forward. Some of these were things that we learnt before the pandemic and were brought into focus as a result of it and others were all new. Learn from our successes but also our failures. Get to where you want to go faster, by using our experiences as a shortcut, rather than having to live them yourself.

We have deliberately written this book as an entire team to provide you with a broad spectrum of personalities, experiences and people, so you can find someone or something that resonates with you. Once you feel a connection with a particular story or team member, pay attention to what they say and test out the same solutions they found useful or alternatively try something completely different. Push your boundaries and believe that change is possible. Because it is.

As individuals, our experiences of the pandemic and its impact have varied enormously, but our reactions and subsequent results of those experiences have been overwhelmingly similar. Because we have a system, a community and the right mindset. Because we are a team.

We want this book to give you those same superpowers, so no matter what the world throws at you, you are resilient enough to not only survive, but thrive. Find your system, find your mindset, find your team.

You may recognise yourself or others in these pages and we hope that will inspire you to act and make a difference. By stepping into our best selves and living our best life, we become the change we want to see in the world. Whilst we might feel insignificant as individuals, our collective powers are boundless, so keep reading and see what differences you might be able to create in your life, for your family and for the world in general.

CHRIS LAMBERT-GORWYN

Chris has been at rock bottom. With more than £100,000 of debt and his first child on the way, he knew something had to change – and fast. He was working every waking hour to provide for his family. But it wasn't working.

His transformative journey started with attending a single sales seminar (which he won't mind telling you, he was very reluctant to attend) and having his eyes opened to what was possible in a heart centred business. He went from a dark financial hole to never having to work another day for money in his life.

Chris and his wife Karene have built multiple 5-, 6- and 7-figure companies, written numerous #1 best-selling business and personal development books and founded the UK's leading business mentorship programme – Passion to Profit for Practitioners (or P2P as we and our clients like to refer to it as).

Humbled by numerous awards, Chris has spoken at business conferences in 14 different countries, spending time with business titans including Sir Richard Branson, Les Brown, Baroness Michelle Mone, Kevin Harrington, Robert Kiyosaki, Tony Robbins and Randi Zuckerberg.

Accolades aside, Chris speaks with passion and candid honesty about both his successes and his failures. Open about his challenges in life and business, he credits a lot of his success to the battle he fought with cancer as a teenager and even goes so far as to say it was one of the best things that ever happened to him.

Chris is the proud father to his 9-year-old daughter Mya and Goldie their maltipoo puppy and has recently achieved his dream of moving his family to live by the beach on the south coast of England.

KARENE LAMBERT-GORWYN

Karene had it all – the money, the title and the status. An incredibly successful corporate career saw her working with numerous multi-national organisations including BMW, BP, ITV as well as the Singapore and UK government all before she'd even blown out the candles on her thirtieth birthday cake.

But following a severe accident that left her unable to work for some time, she started to question whether she was on the right path. So, she left it all behind and forged an entirely new way forward, from scratch.

Karene now once again has it all – but better. Because now she not only has a multi-million-dollar property portfolio that pays her income each month whether she works or not; she also has balance, health, freedom and meaningful relationships.

Alongside husband Chris, she's built multiple 5-, 6- and 7-figure companies as well as the UK's leading business mentorship programme – Passion to Profit for Practitioners.

Through this, they share the systems they used to get themselves where they are today, without sacrificing the things that really matter. And it works. Just ask the 3,000+ business owners who have gone on to thrive after implementing their systems.

These systems have taken Karene from tea at 10 Downing Street to dinner at the House of Lords. She has presented at conferences around the world, rubbing shoulders with Robert and Kim Kiyosaki, Randy Zuckerberg, Baroness Michelle Mone and Karen Brady – to name but a few – and has written numerous business and personal development #1 best-selling books.

Karene shares with passion and honesty the highs – and lows – of business, her experiences as a high-flying woman and how – and why – she chose to change her path. And what life can look like as a business owner, mummy and all those other roles that we pick up along the way.

DAVID GIL-CRISTOBAL
HCB Business Scaling Officer and Serial Entrepreneur

David Gil Cristobal turns people into brands. By putting the correct business systems and structures in place for scalable success, David's clients become the go-to experts in their industry.

He has spent in excess of three decades in the sports and business arena, which has included a career as a professional footballer, founding one of Switzerland's top health & fitness organisations and launching Fitness Fortune University, which builds elite fitness businesses in as little as 90 days.

In 2020 David sold his fitness business, though remains part of it in a consultative role – a service he now offers to the entire industry.

David has personally trained more than 1,000 companies to scale their businesses. The events surrounding the pandemic found him busier than ever, as he put his heart and soul into keeping his fitness industry colleagues and clients afloat.

David has partnered with Chris and Karene numerous times to create new and exciting companies including: HCB Publishing, where they help business owners market themselves to a wider audience so they establish themselves as experts in their field; HCB Words That Work, where individuals and companies are provided words and written materials to move their clients and businesses forward; HCB Speak to Shine, where they train corporate executives and sales teams how to maximise their opportunities and profits; and BeFueld UK, a nutritional supplement and beverage company that fuels active lifestyles.

David holds a Master's degree in Business Management and Leadership, has built multiple 5-, 6- and 7-figure businesses, spoken to more than 100,000 people at business and financial conferences in 13 different countries and on 3 different continents. He is a best-selling author of 7 books in 2 different languages – he himself speaks 6 languages, and has even starred in a film.

ANNA GOODWIN
HCB Managing Director and Head of Mentorship

Managing a rapidly growing team of 14+ employees, supporting more than 250 business mentorship clients at a time and being a full-time mum for her two school age children, Anna Goodwin is the Managing Director of Heart Centred Business. Anna excels at helping people get out of their own way, so that they can get 'unstuck' in their lives and businesses, make a bigger difference in the world and get paid what they're truly worth.

A former Secondary School teacher who left teaching to set up her own successful enterprise, Anna has helped hundreds of women overcome anger and regain a spring in their step. Watching them regain their passion for life and step into their true potential led Anna to bring her expertise to Heart Centred Business so she could impact more people and make a bigger difference. Anna and the Heart Centred Business team support women to create self-reliance in the form of an income, a business and a mindset beyond anything they previously believed to be possible.

AMY ROGERS
HCB Chief Operating Officer

Amy Rogers jumped at the chance to bring her logistical and development skills to Heart Centred Business. Having built successful businesses as an Osteopath and Pilates instructor, she has experienced first-hand the personal and financial growth that is possible when people have mentors, coaches and a system to follow.

Always passionate about making the world a better place, Amy is delighted to do this every day – navigating the systems involved in marketing, sales and delivery, and working internationally with fantastic clients and a world-class team.

DAVID ROYLANCE

HCB Head of Strategy, 'Europe's Smasher of Glass Ceilings' and co-founder of HCB Speak to Shine.

David Roylance is the Head of Mentorship for Chris and Karene's award-winning programme and excels at helping people get results. He has more than 20 years' experience working with FTSE 250 companies, SMEs, entrepreneurs and charities. He was responsible for fast tracking the first woman onto the board of RBS, and has successfully coached many executives to double their income within one week of his input.

Alongside working with his private clients from across Europe, David has been hired by Barclays, Standard Life and Coutts to work with members of their board rooms, and has delivered staff training at HSBC, Macquarie Bank, Zurich Insurance, American Express, Orange, Aviva and Turner Entertainment.

He is known by his clients as Europe's Smasher of Glass Ceilings, and helps his high-level, corporate clients achieve promotions to board-level positions, typically adding an extra £100,000 to their income. Expanding into corporate and team development, David recently partnered with Chris, Karene, and David Gil Cristobal to form HCB Speak to Shine where they teach corporate executives and sales teams how to maximise opportunities and dramatically increase profits.

JANE MCDOWELL

HCB Head of Customer Delight Team, Reflexologist and Massage Therapist

Jane leads the Customer Delight Team at Heart Centred Business, ensuring that all clients feel loved and listened to. In 2019, she won an award for Outstanding Service in her own practice, where she helps people who suffer from migraines. She is passionate about helping other people, is an active community organiser and is on her way to succeeding in her mission to plant 10,000 trees.

Jane has also had a 14-year career in the NHS as a project manager and healthcare planner, working on projects to build new hospitals, dental facilities and relocating emergency services. Her work has brought her in contact with people from all walks of life – above all she loves working with people to help them achieve what sometimes seems impossible.

ALICE COOKE
HCB Head of Content Creation and co-founder of HCB Words That Work
Alice first attended an HCB training in November 2019 – she had a copywriting business that was making very little money despite having a wealth of experience and expertise. Within 3 months of following the HCB system she had tripled her income, and within a year she was running a 6-figure business. That year was 2020. She grew her business exponentially through the start of the pandemic and all the subsequent lockdowns.

She has since taken on multiple associates and moved to a farmhouse on top of a hill (with her dogs Tara and Pom), which gives her mountain views in three directions. She has also gone into partnership with Chris, Karene, and David Gil Cristobal to create HCB Words That Work, to bring her expertise to more companies looking to increase their client numbers and grow their revenue. To say that Alice's life has completely changed for the better during the pandemic would almost be something of an understatement.

SARAH HAMON WATT
HCB Operations and Sales, and Personal Fitness Trainer
Sarah is a keen runner and weightlifter and works in the HCB Operations and Sales Teams, meaning she handles the behind-the-scenes organisation of the company, alongside sales conversations with potential clients to explore if HCB is the right company to help them achieve their goals.

Having joined HCB as a client herself in 2019, using the system she was taught, Sarah grew her international, mobile personal training company from an idea to a £10k a month business employing two members of staff. Specialising in pre- and post-natal fitness, Sarah helps women become the fittest and strongest version of themselves. She empowers them through movement, mindset and nutrition to enhance their recovery and safely achieve more than they ever imagined.

SHARON BETTERTON
HCB Customer Delight Team, and Sports Massage Therapist
Sharon was a brilliant secretary – efficient, knowledgeable and hard working. But she wasn't happy. She had once trained as a sports massage therapist and longed to put that training to good use. So, when she and her family decided to move out of London, she seized her chance to start her own business. However, she didn't really believe it could work full time and merely aimed to make 'pocket money' to support her household. Unfortunately, she struggled to find any clients and spent a lot of money on magazine adverts that didn't work which reinforced her belief that she couldn't build a business.

Fortunately, since working with HCB as a client, Sharon's mindset and skill set have dramatically improved and her business income tripled. But then a few years ago Sharon had an accident on her bike that left her with life changing injuries and a lot of trauma. Struggling physically, her confidence took a huge hit. It has made her a quieter, more self-conscious person, who, in her own words, "wouldn't say boo to a goose".

Many months of hard work later, Sharon is in the process of becoming the Sharon she used to be – and it's working. From refusing to raise her hand at events and crying when asked to speak in front of a room, Sharon now hosts and runs entirely online events for HCB. She is a valued member of the HCB team and an inspiration to everyone she meets.

PREFACE

Our business is changing lives. We do this by taking everything we've learnt on our journey and teaching it to our clients, so that they can achieve success too. This might be in business, finances or relationships – the principles are the same. We teach people how to change the way they think, so that they can become self-reliant, create a different reality for themselves and have a greater impact on the world.

This has never been more relevant than it is now. In the wake (and continued waves and repercussions) of the coronavirus pandemic, business has changed. Our attitudes to business have changed, the way we do business and expect to do business with others, has changed. So, we must change too, or risk being left behind altogether. Life has thrown us all a curveball, but rather than see it as a crisis, we challenge you to see it as an opportunity.

You might already be feeling some resistance to this idea, great, take note of it as it is a key learning too. And, if you want to throw a tantrum and vent about your situation this is healthy too and most of the team I (Karene), at some point, have certainly thrown a few tantrums, then, we pick ourselves up, work out what happens next and keep going.

The ten topics that form the basis of this book are challenges we all face, regardless of our age, background or experience. We have all at some stage in our lives felt not as good as someone else, not sure of ourselves, not enough – and this is where the questions spread throughout this book come in. Because, for the most part, the only obstacle in your way is you. The questions and topics in this book will help you find a way forward and turn challenges into opportunities.

Fundamentally, it's about how you react when the going gets tough. Who do you become when you're unsure, challenged, or pushed into a corner? Whatever the answer is, is that person going to help you move forward, or are they holding you back? Are you taking steps towards the life you want to live every day, or are you just existing? Perhaps you may even be hiding?

We want this book to show you what's possible for you, by approaching the issues you face every day in a different way. Once you've discovered what success means for you, we want you to go and get it – and start to change your reality, today.

There is always more – more happiness, more freedom, more love, more money. Take the points that will make the most difference for you – to your business, your happiness, and your life. As we and our team share the ways in which they have taken control of the quality of their lives and adapted, we hope you will be inspired and/or driven to do the same.

If you're serious about moving your life or business forward in some way, and the fact that you're reading this book tells us that this applies to you, consider that whenever you do something new or different – whether it be learning a skill or approaching life from a different angle to take you to another level – getting a mentor is one of the quickest routes to success. A mentor is someone who has done it before, someone whose story, values and goals resonate with our own. Someone who will show you from experience, not theory, how to shortcut success and create new experiences more powerfully and more effectively. Mentors are a key element to any success and can range from your parents to your sports coaches, from a helpful boss to a successful entrepreneur. If you want to succeed more quickly in anything, find an expert in that area who has a system to teach you so you can learn from their mistakes.

Mentors are how Karene and I (Chris) created our success, and, in particular, how I turned financial ruin into lifetime financial security. Primarily, this is why we created the businesses we have – to share with others what has worked so well for us. To date, we have shown over 3,000 people how to create massive success. The business systems we teach and continue to use ourselves always include mindset, systems and community, which are themes that will come up throughout this book. You can have the best business systems in the world, but unless you are able to get out of your own way, to implement them effectively, you have no business. Why? Because you are your business! If your mindset, health, energy levels or belief systems are not in the right place, it doesn't matter what strategies you use, none of them will work. And that's the case whether you are a business owner looking to grow, an employee hoping for promotion, or a parent wanting to stay calm despite the stress and challenges of raising children and running a household!

You must manage how you show up, to manage your life. And this is true in business just as it is in any other area you want to succeed in.

HOW TO GET THE MOST OUT OF THIS BOOK...

You can either enjoy reading this passively: you will get insight into our lives and why we have created the success we have. Or actively: from a place of curiosity and intrigue as to how you could apply these stories and actions into your own life. If you engage and challenge your way of thinking you might just create the results you are looking for! Your choice.

At the end of every section there are suggested actions to take because it is action, not thoughts, that will move you forward. Thought without action is just dreaming. Thought combined with effective action can change the entire world. So, decide, here and now, what level of change you want in your life.

Will you take the actions like your life depends on it? Because if you think about it, it does!

Or will this just be another 'nice to have' book on the shelf that entertains you for a while before you continue on as before?

You get to choose. Just like you get to choose every action that either moves you forward to the life you want or holds you back. Without action, nothing changes. If you read this book and put the ideas presented into action, who knows what sort of life you could create for yourself? Chris and I (Karene) are still exploring this concept ourselves and have created a more joy-packed life than we ever could have imagined. And every day, we still get to choose whether our actions will move us forward or backwards. We all have this choice, whether we like it or not, and we hope this book gives you some motivation and ideas of how different choices and actions could lead to a very different life!

CONTENTS

1 - Life either happens to you or for you: you create your reality   **1**

When we change the way we look at things, the things we look at change
– Wayne Dyer

2 - Do the right things in the right order   **9**

If you always do what you've always done, you'll always get what you've
always gotten – Tony Robbins

3 - Success Conditioning: Rituals for Life   **17**

What is important is seldom urgent and what is urgent is seldom important
– Dwight D. Eisenhower

4 - You can't pour from an empty cup: help yourself first   **23**

On an aeroplane they tell you to put your oxygen mask on before helping
others. The same thinking applies in life – if you don't help yourself first,
you won't be able to help others – Chris Lambert-Gorwyn

5 - Energy is key!   **29**

Few ever drop dead from overwork, but many quietly curl up and die
because of under-satisfaction – Sidney J. Harris

6 - A supportive community is key! Surround yourself with the right people   **39**

We are the average of the five people we spend the most time with – Jim Rohn

7 - Know your 'why' and connect with what you really want   **45**

Nothing can stop a man with the right mental attitude from achieving his
goal; nothing on Earth can help the man with the wrong mental attitude
– Thomas Jefferson

8 - Turning your dreams into reality: create a plan   55

People with goals succeed because they know where they're going
– Earl Nightingale

9 - Without action, nothing changes!   65

Inaction brings fear and doubt, action brings momentum – Napoleon Hill

10 - Bouncebackability' ...also known as resilience   73

Every winner has scars – Herbert Casson

CHAPTER 1

LIFE EITHER HAPPENS TO YOU OR FOR YOU: YOU CREATE YOUR REALITY

When we change the way we look at things,
the things we look at change.
– Wayne Dyer

Even in the most challenging of times we have a choice. We can choose what to do and we can choose how to feel. 2020 and 2021 took away some of those choices, or seemed to. And as a result, changed all our lives. But our lives do not have to be dictated by our circumstances. Even in the midst of life challenges – when it may seem like we have no choice – we always do!

Take a moment to ask yourself right now:
What would a great life look like,
regardless of the circumstances?

Are you taking action to change the world around you, or merely reacting to what happens? Are you being a 'victim' of your circumstance or creating your reality?

More often than not, this is a question of how you choose to see things. A constant for all of us is that life happens; things go wrong, things go right. And how you choose to react – and act – when life happens, is the difference between success and failure.

With the Pandemic, remembering that you have a choice is something that we may have all needed a reminder of. Certainly, there have been 'mandates' as to what is or isn't acceptable and also a lot of grey areas. We all know that people have railed against being told what to do and many who have complied and complained and many who have adjusted and carried on. This is the 'reaction' that we get to choose.

Just ask David Roylance, our co-founder at HCB Speak to Shine and HCB's Head of Strategy. He is a classically trained actor, who when at drama school rubbed shoulders (and in some cases shared a flat) with Ewan McGregor, Joseph Fiennes and Damian Lewis. They are all huge Hollywood stars who 'made it' – but David didn't (not as an actor, anyway).

He struggled with this for a long time. In fact, it really got him down and affected the way he felt, acted and reacted to the world around him. He thought: 'Why them? Why not me?'

The turning point for David came when he discovered personal development. Having attended an event hosted by American author Darren Hardy, he then read his book, *The Compound Effect*. This led him to watch presentations by Tony Robbins and Andy Harrington. Through hearing their experiences, he got on board with the concept of looking at things differently. He realised that he had 'made it' he was just judging himself by the wrong criteria. It was then that he found us at

HCB, and we are very much about looking at the world in a positive way – or rather, looking in a way that will move you forward. You cannot control what happens to you, but you can control how you react to it.

He realised that the way he was looking at events over which he had no control was what was making him miserable – not the events themselves. And the way you choose to look at things is something that you have absolute control over.

By changing his mindset, David was able to change the way he looked at the world. Now, as an incredibly successful entrepreneur, who we count ourselves lucky to have as part of our business, his mindset has done a complete 180°. He now thinks: 'Who can I help today? What have I learnt from this? – and what can I teach other people as a result of having learnt that?'

This constant questioning to force a change in perspective regardless of what is going on, is exactly how he's managed to achieve so much. He changed the way he looked at the world around him, and the world around him changed.

How do you look at the world around you? Do you feel that life's been hard on you? That others have been dealt better cards? How could you look at this in a different way?

Sometimes even when you are looking at the world differently it can all get too much. Have you ever been close to 'burn-out'? And by that we mean reaching a point where you felt you couldn't carry on. Because if you have ... you did manage to carry on, because you're still here. In order to get out of that state of mind, not only did you have to see things differently but you also had to do something differently. So, you already have that ability. You just have to remember it, channel it and believe that you can.

If you have ever felt burnt out, then you're certainly not alone. Anna Goodwin, our Managing Director, had a change in mindset brought about as a direct result of the pandemic. In fact, the pandemic changed her mindset for the worse, before she realised what was happening and managed to change it for the better.

In March 2020, as coronavirus reared its ugly head in earnest, Anna had more than 200 mentees to support – all worried for their health, their businesses and the unknown. What was going to happen next? They didn't know and neither did Anna. But as Managing Director of the company, she felt a huge responsibility to help each and every one of them personally, over 200 of them.

This would have been a huge burden to carry in anyone's books (which Anna felt it was her duty to carry), but add to that the fact she was also homeschooling her two children, who were themselves unsure about what was happening and what might happen next. Again, Anna could have asked for help with this, but felt she didn't need to. She was superwoman!

Except, as much as we love her, she wasn't. This was all too much for one person to carry. And she didn't need to be carrying it alone. She didn't want to let go of the control though – not at home and not at work.

But as so often happens (and this in itself is a great lesson to learn), there needed to be a bit of a breakdown, in order for there to be a breakthrough. Whilst none of us like this experience, it also just makes sense: in order to re-create something in a different way, you must break it apart first. Anytime a breakdown happens in our lives or business, it is actually a perfect opportunity to make changes and create a different reality going forward. Life either happens to you, or it happens for you: your choice will determine your experience!

The day Anna asked for help, was the day Anna got help – from the HCB Team, from her family and from her friends. Her fear of letting go of control was holding her back. The moment she let go of some of that control, she learned (or perhaps remembered) the value of teamwork – at home and at HCB. She didn't need to do everything alone, and neither do you.

And I (Karene) am guilty of this myself. I used to be massively independent. In fact, it was a lot more extreme than that – I needed to be in control of everything, it was my way of protecting myself from hurt. But that wasn't making me happy. Because you can never be in control of everything and attempting to means that you don't let anyone in so your relationships suffer not to mention the stress and overwhelm. None of us is an island and we all work better together.

Many of us are resistant to letting go or sharing because it hasn't always worked in the past. That however is not a guarantee of the future. You can and should ask for help or at the very least let people know what is going on for you. If they can't support you directly they may allow you to look at things differently. I have found that explaining something to others can sometimes provide that 'different way of looking at things' that then allows you to realise that you aren't alone and that there is always another way.

And looking at this another way, if you never share what is going on for you, you'll never give the gift of allowing someone else to help and we all know how good that feels so if you can't do it for yourself, do it for someone else.

Being independent and in control of everything is considered a strength – especially in the corporate world – but it's actually a weakness. Independence, may perpetuate a feeling of control but it also keeps things small. Businesses don't grow when leaders don't share the load. We could never have supported the mentees that we have or changed as many lives if Chris and I (Karene) just kept doing everything ourselves.

Think of a successful person. They could be a public figure or someone that you know personally. All successful people have had help to get to where they are now. And that doesn't make their success any less deserved – it just made it easier to obtain. Why wouldn't you want to make things easier for yourself? You won't be any more successful if you struggle and do everything by yourself. In fact, you're far more likely to fail if you go about things like that. Why increase your chance of failure?

You will get to where you want to get to a lot quicker if you recognise that there is strength in asking for help.

Where in your life are you holding on too tightly?
Where could you ask for help?

ACTION POINTS

1. Go back and look at things you consider to be your past failures. Think of them instead as learnings – how does that change your perception of that event? How could you have reacted differently? What actions could you have taken that might have made those experiences less painful or even turned them into an opportunity? What if everything that happened to you was exactly what you needed to be successful? You had to go through it all in order to become who you need to be. Notice what you could have done differently. Then decide, right here and now, how you might choose to react differently if something similar happened again.

2. And on the other hand, what in your life do you need to let go of? Where in your life are you worrying about what everybody thinks and letting a fear of judgement hold you back? What would you do today if you didn't have that fear? Where in your life are you not letting go of control? Who could you ask to help you, that might mean you could have more time, and could achieve more? What's stopping you from asking them?

3. Think again of that successful person we asked you to think of just now. What is it that makes you think they're successful? What do they have what you want? What qualities do you admire in them? You can have what they have, in both instances, you just need to decide what exactly it is that you want. Be clear, think in detail about what you want. Write down all your thoughts on this because the act of writing things down, starts the process of making it happen.

CHAPTER 2

DO THE RIGHT THINGS IN THE RIGHT ORDER

If you always do what you've always done,
you'll always get what you've always gotten.
– Tony Robbins

This isn't just about doing the right thing for your business – it's about doing what's right for your business right now, and having a plan of action. That plan of action should be your map – your guide to follow. Then you must stick to it. Which sounds easy but isn't – it's quite the opposite. It's uncomfortable, and hard, and at times not very enjoyable. But if you keep doing what you're doing now, nothing will change.

> How long have you been trying to do
> things the way you are doing them now?
> What results has that got you?
> What results do you want it to get you?

Einstein once said: "Insanity is doing the same thing over and over again and expecting different results."

This 'doing the right things in the right order' theme is a thread that runs throughout this book, so let it come as no surprise when it comes up again and again – that's how important it is. Get it right and you'll get results, no matter in what area of life and business.

So how do we go about doing things in the right order?

It's as simple as:

- Get a goal
- Get a map (a plan, a guide or a mentor)
- Get a new mindset

Which looks simple, but in practice is really quite challenging. By getting a goal you'll know where you're going, which will in turn give you a renewed focus. By getting a map or a mentor, you'll know the route to take, how to prepare, and what to watch out for along the way. And the new mindset will ensure that you keep moving forward by keeping your goal in mind ensuring that you can and will achieve the goal you set.

How?

By taking action.

Sounds scary?

Good. In order to take action, you need to change your mindset – if you don't, you'll be too paralysed by fear to do anything, and you won't be able to move forward.

Feel the fear and do it anyway.

Because in order to move yourself forward from where you are, you are going to have to do things differently. And because they are different, they aren't familiar, or comfortable. Which is why you need to have the right mindset. Fix your focus on what exactly it is you want to achieve, and then know that every uncomfortable step you take now is taking you one step closer to that end result.

Each small step is important.

Every small step moves you forward. Lots of small steps add up to make massive change and progress. Don't let yourself feel overwhelmed by the end goal, let it inspire you, and know that you can move towards it every day, one small step at a time. Don't be afraid to do things differently.

What is your end goal?
What small step could you take today
to get you closer to that goal?

We truly can live the life we've always dreamed about, regardless of anything that's happening around us, if we understand that the external world is not the driving force behind who we become or what we create.

The biggest trap that keeps people from taking action is fear – fear of failure, fear of success, fear of rejection, fear of pain, fear of the unknown. The only way to deal with fear is to face it – to go through it. That way to move forward is to learn the hard lessons, so that you can come out the other side better than you were when you went in.

As humans we do more to avoid pain than we will ever do to gain pleasure. For most of us, avoiding pain is the greater motivator. By changing your focus, you instantly transform.

What would a great life look like for you, regardless of the circumstances?

For Sarah Hamon Watt, HCB's Head of Logistics, the dream was to leave the gym she was connected to and start working for herself full time as a Personal Trainer. Which she did – in the middle of the pandemic. She went from working two and a half days a week in a gym, to driving round with her equipment in the boot of her car doing personal training sessions full time – then she went online from home.

In fact, thanks to the support of her community, 2020 was actually her best year ever financially. She doubled her income, left her job in the gym and launched her own business. All because she was reminded what was possible and did the right things in the right order to make it happen. She went from working incredibly hard for very little reward, to working exclusively for herself. Not only that, but she now has two associates working for her.

She was able to do this because she had a map to follow and was able to learn from experts who had already done what she wanted to do – she didn't need to make mistakes, she learnt from theirs. This meant she was able to succeed far more quickly than others in her position.

Was it plain sailing all the way? Absolutely not. Sarah most definitely had to face her fears head on. But she remained focused on her goal and where she wanted to be.

What change have you been
thinking about but not doing? What's stopping you?
Remember, everything you want is on the other side of fear.

Alice Cooke, co-founder of HCB Words That Work and Head of Content Creation at HCB, had a similar experience, in as much as she was copywriting in the evenings for friends and family and enjoying that a lot more than her full-time job as a journalist. So, she left. She left the security of a full-time role, paid holidays, a pension scheme and an office, and set up on her own.

When she first started out, she took a part-time job in events to make ends meet. But then March 2020 rolled around and there were no events anymore, so she was made redundant. At this point she had a choice – like we all have choices, in everything we do. She could go back to the safety and security of journalism, or she could make life a lot harder for herself in the short term and follow her dream.

She took the path less trodden and set up on her own. But in the first few months she earnt very little money – she found it really very difficult and struggled to pay her bills. But she kept going. She kept believing in herself, even though she was told frequently that it wasn't a good time to start a business.

She now earns three times what she was earning in her journalism role, working for herself, from home, on her own terms. She achieved this by facing her fear head on and having a supportive community behind her. But the real point of difference is that Alice did absolutely everything we told her to do, without deviation and without any omissions. She had total and utter faith in the system and kept taking action – as a result it worked for her very quickly and continues to work for her every day. She did the right things, in the right order.

What stops you from doing the right things in the right order more often than not is everyone's opinions. Everybody has an opinion on what you should or should not do. But if you take everybody's advice, you'll end up trying to do everything and nothing will work. You need to commit to one course of action and drown out all other noise. If you're following a tried and tested system, have absolute faith that it will work – because it will, but only if you take action and follow the system.

> **Where do you want to get to?**
> **If you don't know where you want to go,**
> **then it doesn't matter what you do,**
> **because you won't get anywhere**
> **except where you are right now.**

To achieve anything in life, you need to focus and do the right things in the right order. But to know what the right things are for you, you need to know where you want to get to.

ACTION POINTS

1. Get clear on where you are. Where are you in the world? Who are you surrounding yourself with? Where are you starting from and where do you want to get to? What is the gap?

    See things as they are, rather than better or worse than they are. If you're clear on where you are now, it'll help you get clear on what areas of life you want to make changes in.

    What are the top 3 areas you'd like to change? Maybe your finances? Your business? Your relationships?

2. Do you have a map, a guide and a community? If not, get one. Find someone who has bridged the gap in the area(s) that you are changing, because success leaves clues. Learn from other people's mistakes so you don't have to make as many mistakes yourself.

3. Consider following a single path, rather than many at once – it will help you stay laser focused and prevent you from taking the easy and longer way round when fear gets in your way. What will move you forward right here and now even if it's not a comfortable or pleasant step to take?

CHAPTER 3

SUCCESS CONDITIONING: RITUALS FOR LIFE

*What is important is seldom urgent
and what is urgent is seldom important.*
– Dwight D. Eisenhower

If you win the morning, you win the day! Wouldn't it be great to have a 10/10 day more often? Lots of highly successful people start each morning with a routine. But it's not just the routine that helps you win the day. Attitude is everything.

How you do anything is how you do everything. When you use your mental attitude to your advantage, it is a very powerful asset. Having the wrong mindset – such as telling yourself you can't do something, or that you're not good enough – is setting yourself up to fail.

**What is your morning routine?
How could you change it to better set you up for success?**

The first hour of every day is key to establishing your mood, your mindset and your positivity for the rest of the day. Whatever your morning routine currently looks like, making even little improvements will help set you up with the right mental attitude to have a more successful day.

It was that good mental attitude, created by consistent daily rituals, that David Roylance credits with "saving him" at the beginning of 2020. Like so many businesses, his business took a huge financial hit in 2020, but he was determined that his positive mindset wouldn't suffer a similar blow. He had to be flexible, vigilant, willing to change and learn to keep the money coming in. But to do all that he had to get himself in the right frame of mind.

His first new ritual was to take up running before work. He found that this woke him up, allowed him to gain perspective on his worries and see the bigger picture, which meant he was able to move his business forward every single day. After that he would repeat a number of affirmations – where he wanted to get to, in what timeframe and how – in very specific terms. Then, and only then, was he ready to face the day. In fact, he still does all this now – and he will keep on doing it and be all the better for having established all these new rituals.

But David didn't take up running to move his business forward, he took up running because he got some very scary news – this ritual really did save him. At a routine health check, he was told he was on the brink of diabetes, and that if he didn't do something about it in a hurry, he would be put on high doses of medication and was on track for even more serious implications for his health.

Even having been given that shocking diagnosis though, David needed a mindset shift in order to take action. Initially he was appalled that his body could have let him down in such a way – but then he realised it was quite the opposite, he had let his body down. So, he got into action and did something about it – every single day.

He, like so many of us through the pandemic, was faced with a situation that might well have overwhelmed him, were it not for the actions he took to help move him forward. Had he stopped and taken no action, the consequences could have been far more serious – for his business and his life.

For his business to survive through the pandemic and in the long term, he had to change the way he worked, the way he marketed himself, the people he spoke to and the way he showed up in every conversation. He credits his rituals for allowing him to be flexible enough to work in a new way – and being open to the possibility that there may yet be another new way of working. His rituals ground him, focus him and allow him to see clearly. For that reason, they have become a non-negotiable part of his day – for his health, his well-being and his business.

And the consequences of this? David has lost massive amounts of weight, feels better, looks better, has a lot more energy and was recently told by his doctor that he no longer has and is not at risk of having diabetes. Quite a win from simply changing his mindset and creating rituals to start his day differently!

Where could you take a new set of actions or establish new rituals to move you forward?

Like David, we discovered (or perhaps rediscovered) the importance of rituals for ourselves when we were writing our best-selling book

Grow Your Heart Centred Business. The book was designed to help more people create better results so they can make a bigger difference in the world – and when the pandemic hit, this desire was brought even more sharply into focus.

It was incredibly hard, and we don't mind telling you that we were exhausted. We were pushing ourselves to the limits of what we could fit into every day (and night) to get the book over the line. We were still presenting at events, running courses, providing mentorship and support for our 200+ current clients, running our multiple other businesses as well as looking after our daughter, Mya, and managing a team of people – who we felt a huge responsibility for.

This meant very little sleep, it meant pushing social engagements and free time aside and doing 20-hour days for the month we took to write our book. Then, when we had sent the book to the publisher and thought we could sit back and recover, the pandemic hit and the all-consuming pace continued so we could support our team and our clients through the challenging times.

Yes, we could have chosen a different approach, both to writing our book, and to supporting our clients and team through the pandemic. 20-hour days are not our preference! Yet, the goal we were focused on more than justified being uncomfortable for a short period of time. We had talked about writing a book for years and done nothing. By committing to creating a book within a very limited timeframe, we made it happen and created a best-seller. By putting in the extra time and support for our clients during the pandemic, many of them had the best year financially that they've ever had.

In order to achieve so much in each day though, we had to be incredibly disciplined, and we had to make sure that we won every day right from the very start. This meant putting ourselves in the right frame of mind, sticking to the routine that we found most useful and taking one small step at a time, instead of looking at the enormity of the project as a whole. We established a morning routine that involved getting outside and exercising, eating properly, drinking lots of water, meditating and listening to our favourite music on repeat, all before we started the day. By doing all this, we made sure we were alert, focused on the outcome, positive and ready to take action and able to continue for far longer each day than we otherwise would have been able to.

If you can succeed at sticking to your routine, you have already succeeded before the day has even got going, so you're setting yourself up for further success.

Instead of fearing change – in routine, in circumstances, in the world – try looking at life differently. Embrace it and try to think of ways in which you might turn everything that happens into an opportunity.

If you don't keep coming back to why you are doing everything that you're doing, life will get in your way. Except it won't be life that stops you, it'll be you. Create a routine and a structure to your day that will serve you. And be flexible with it too – know when your routine is helping you, and when it might need to change slightly or move around a bit in order to help you make the most of your day. Your routine and your rituals should always be there to help, not hinder you. Don't get too caught up in what your day *should* look like, or even what success *should* look like. Instead stay focused on your goals and adapt each day based on what life throws at you so you can keep moving forwards.

ACTION POINTS

1. What does your morning routine consist of? What works and what doesn't? What do you need to change to make sure you win the day?

2. When things don't go as you planned or thought they might, what routines or rituals do you have in place to get you back on track? Is there a particular piece of music you could play? Would a walk help? What smells make you think of positive, productive things? Have a bag of mood/state changers at your disposal and know which ones work best for you – short-term and long-term.

3. What rituals do you need to introduce to your day? What reminders do you need to say (or not say), to make sure your attitude – to the day, to your clients, to life – is exactly where it needs to be.

CHAPTER 4

YOU CAN'T POUR FROM AN EMPTY CUP: HELP YOURSELF FIRST

On an aeroplane they tell you to put your own oxygen mask on
first before helping others. The same thinking applies in life –
if you're not ok, you won't be any use to other people.
– Chris Lambert-Gorwyn

This is an idea that many of us are resistant to. Surely being heart-centred
and a good person means helping others instead of yourself?

Yes and no.

You cannot pour from an empty cup. You cannot help other people
from a position of burnout, worry, stress or scarcity. Similarly, if you're
feeling dejected, angry or you're blaming yourself (or other people)
for everything, your cup is already full, and you aren't able to give
as fully or effectively to others.

It's the same concept as putting on your own oxygen mask on a plane,
before putting on that of a child. Or what they teach in lifeguarding which
is to not put yourself in danger when trying to rescue someone else,

otherwise you just end up with two people needing rescuing.

To be of maximum service to other people, you need to be in a safe position to be able to help. Without your own oxygen mask on, you're not going to be much use to anyone else long term.

> **What's in your cup and how full is it?**
> **What are you holding on to, or approaching**
> **everyday life with, that is not putting you in the**
> **best position to help others?**
> **What do you need to do to change that?**

With positivity and a sense of calm and focus in your cup, instead of overwhelmingness and fatigue, it's amazing what you can create. When you're dejected, angry, bored or uninspired (or a not-very-nice combination of more than one of those) you'll get entirely different results. However, blaming yourself when things don't go the way you planned is not the definition of being responsible, it's actually just beating yourself up and it won't help.

> **Where in your life do you give yourself a hard time?**
> **And where has this got you so far?**

Sharon Betterton, part of the Customer Delight Team at HCB, used to be the queen of beating herself up – self-effacing doesn't quite cover it. She was backward in coming forward, to put it mildly. She much preferred standing at the back of the room, would never volunteer to speak in front of anyone, and was quite happy not being noticed at all. You can imagine how useful that was – or rather was not – in building her business.

And all that was before she had a cycling accident that put her out of action for the best part of a year and threatened to completely shatter what little confidence she had. But that didn't happen – quite the opposite, in fact.

'Coming out of her shell' wouldn't quite do Sharon's transformation over this past year justice. From someone who would shake and nearly cry (her words not ours) when asked to address a room, she can now (and has) led entire meetings of delegates – which included fielding questions, issuing directions and even getting everyone up and dancing at various points.

Not only that but Sharon is physically stronger than she's ever been and is now able to do so much more – both in work terms but also with her son. How did she manage all this? By taking the time to look after herself and making her own needs a priority. Only by doing this was she able to give more, and as such she perfectly exemplifies what it means to look after yourself first, so that you are more able to look after others.

Sharon has learnt to look after herself in a more effective way and is now able to be a better version of herself as a result.

Where in life or business have you not looked after yourself, or kept yourself stuck?
Have you considered that by putting yourself first you might be able to create far greater results for your clients and the people you love?

Perhaps before you answer those questions it would help you to hear a bit more about Alice, who used to have a habit of doing this differently – often to her own detriment. Alice is an incredibly kind, giving person. In fact, you could argue that she gives too much. She is there for everyone in her life, no matter what it costs her personally. In her business, Alice's clients absolutely love working with her because they knew that no matter what they asked, or at what time of day, Alice would support them and deliver whatever they needed – even if it meant pulling all-nighters so she didn't let anyone else down while she went above and beyond for them. No one knew the pressure she put on herself – all they saw was the outstanding results she created in unworkable timeframes, time and time again. The thing is, how sustainable or realistic is it to work like this? Imagine how exhausting it would be?!

As the coronavirus pandemic swept the planet, when her friends, family and clients needed more help and support than ever, Alice was going through her own personal crisis with a relationship break-up, moving across the country and trying to build a business that was working her into the ground. Whilst outwardly all seemed good and her business was going from strength to strength, Alice was personally struggling. This is the very definition of pouring from an empty cup. If you don't look after yourself first, you have so much less to give. You can give more by helping yourself first.

Realising she was close to burn out, Alice shifted how she did things. With the pandemic forcing her clients to reassess their usual methods of operating, Alice progressively stepped into more of a leadership role when dealing with them. First, she started saying "No" to things, which absolutely terrified her initially because she thought she would lose all her clients. However, by saying "No" to jobs that were time consuming, low paid and which she didn't really want to do anyway, she freed up her time to focus on clients who provided more interesting and better-paid projects. She also found, to her surprise, that when she said "No" to people or expressed the need for a different or slower time frame than they requested, most of the time, her clients were totally fine with it and willing to fit in with her availability. Yes, of course there will always be some urgent projects that need completing ASAP, but by being clear on what is possible and what isn't, Alice's schedule started to open up, so she could provide the necessary flexibility without having to pull all-nighters to fit everything in.

Along with saying "No", Alice also started asking more questions to better understand the overall outcome that her clients wanted. This meant she could understand where in the bigger picture an individual piece of work sat, meaning she and the clients could better determine its relative importance and real timeframe of implementation. This not only provided more balance in her work diary, but it also helped her clients from a strategic point of view, as Alice helped them determine what actions would move their business forward rather than her service being a 'nice-to-have'. By providing greater service to her clients, she is better able to look after herself and Alice has also made herself more valuable. She went from a struggling start-up to a six-figure business during 2020, when the pandemic was in full force.

Stepping into being a leader rather than just saying "Yes" created a better work structure for Alice, with happier clients and a rapidly increasing revenue. This has led to a better work–life balance – she has time to look after herself and is providing a better and better service to her clients, as she finds she has more to give.

Where in life do you need to learn to say "No"?
When you consider this, do you hear a little voice telling you
that you're being selfish?
This voice is not telling the truth.
It is selfish to deplete your reserves trying to help everyone
because it means you actually have less to give.
Take a step back and look after you and you will be more able
to take care of others.

ACTION POINTS

1. Where in your life do you feel resentful that you are giving too much? What are you doing (or not doing) for yourself that would change this feeling right now?

2. What are you focusing on? If it doesn't bring you joy, stop doing it. Find something that does bring you joy so you can be 'recharged'.

3. If what you're doing isn't working, think about how you could change your approach and do things differently in order to create a different outcome for yourself. Then make a plan, take action to create a permanent change.

CHAPTER 5

ENERGY IS KEY!

Few ever drop dead from overwork, but many quietly
curl up and die because of under-satisfaction.
– Sidney J. Harris

Have you ever wondered how some people just seem to have endless
energy, regardless of what is going on in their world? Energy is the
secret ingredient that makes everything else just seem to work better.
If you had more energy, you'd be able to do more, concentrate longer,
work harder – live more.

Simply put, having more energy makes everything easier, meaning
success (in every area of life) suddenly becomes more attainable.

**When was the last time you
felt you were flying high with energy?
What had you done or what happened
to create that energy?**

Energy can make or break how you take on the world. When you have
it, you feel great, and you feel like anything is possible (which it kind

of is). When you don't have it, it can feel like everything is a struggle and a push – everything is hard and challenging.

Energy is that special ingredient that makes everything else work better. If you had more energy, you'd be able to do more, concentrate for longer, work harder, live more. Very simply, having more energy means everything becomes easier and success in every area of life becomes more likely. Whereas not having enough energy, makes everything feel like hard work and more challenging.

Energy is the underappreciated magic that makes or breaks everything else in life. And yet, increasing our energy levels, like losing weight, is actually very simple. Whilst there are entire mountains of science and research into how energy works and how we can increase our energy levels, fundamentally we all forget how simple it really is…

Do more of what gives you energy
and less of what depletes it.

It isn't any more complicated than this, yet, like so many things in life, it's almost like we can't believe it could be this simple.

So, what will give you energy?

The list is endless and includes the obvious, such as sleep, healthy food, exercise, breathing, and meditation; as well as the less obvious and less scientifically recognised, such as laughter, friendship, spiritual connection, living with purpose, and love.

And what will deplete your energy?

Sometimes our energy is depleted by the simple absence of things that give us energy, such as a lack of sleep or not eating healthy food. However, there are also specific things that deplete our energy levels in overt and/or covert ways, such as negative thought patterns, gossip-style or negative conversations, financial concerns and money worries, fear, unhappy romantic relationships, incomplete tasks, too many tasks or boredom.

I (Chris) know only too well what it's like to have no energy. Not just low energy where you feel a bit run down, or struggle to get up in the morning; but the complete absence of energy so your mind and body feels completely shut down. Even a single flight of stairs would leave me gasping and having to sit down to recover; and a simple 5-minute conversation would be a huge mental challenge leaving me exhausted with my brain struggling to keep up with what was being said.

I (Chris) struggled with Chronic Fatigue Syndrome, also known as CFS or ME, for several years and was unable to work. Sometimes I couldn't even get out of bed.

Life became a constant battle of trying to preserve and build my energy so I could complete even the simplest of activities. I tried anything and everything to restore my energy levels with mixed success. However, over several years, I slowly grew to learn the simple truth: when I simply did more of what gave me energy each day and less of what depleted it, I made progress and felt better. It wasn't consistent and didn't always follow a clear pattern but as long as each day I did more things that boosted my energy, slowly and progressively over months and years, I recovered.

Trying to continue living my life the way it was before getting sick and just trying to push through the 'weakness' didn't work. Then again, neither did just resigning myself to being sick and having no energy. Instead, having a daily focus on what built energy and a daily awareness of what depleted it, had the biggest impact over time.

The startling thing I discovered was that it wasn't always the obvious things that made the biggest difference.

Negative conversations:

I started to notice that some of my friends and people I spent time with had a very negative outlook on life and every conversation with them left me drained. Once I recognised this, I consciously chose to limit my interactions with these people and started spending more time in conversations with people who had a more positive outlook on life. The more I did this, the less 'drained' I felt after social interactions.

Filling my mind:

Paying attention to what I filled my mind with each day, such as the books I read, the movies and TV I watched, and the social media I interacted with, made a huge difference. I noticed the more I filled my mind with things that inspired me or made me curious, or caused me to laugh, the better I felt.

Toxic relationships:

Recognising and finally admitting to myself how dysfunctional and traumatic my first marriage was and that we had to separate and get divorced for both of our sakes was not an easy realisation. Whilst the break-up and ensuing divorce was very painful and stressful, it also removed a huge drain on my energy levels as I finally stopped living in fear and started being true to myself and my own feelings. The self-awareness that came from this paved the way for the fulfilling and supportive relationship I now treasure with my wife Karene.

Having purpose and finding fulfilment:

Coming to terms with what I loved about my work and also what I hated about it allowed me to identify what I needed long term. Getting up each morning with drive and purpose compared with dreading the day to come, is like night and day in terms of energy levels. As I progressively did more and more of what made my eyes 'shine' my energy levels expanded equally.

Laughing:

Children laugh more than adults. And they have a LOT more energy. There's an obvious connection and fortunately science is just now catching up and proving that laughter has a host of benefits such as improving our immune systems, increasing cognitive alertness, improving facial muscle tone and increasing our general sense of well-being, including our energy levels.

Personally, I started noticing that on days when I laughed, I felt better and had more energy. So, I made a point to laugh more by watching or listening to comedies, having fun with friends and playing games. Sounds pretty simple, but then the best solutions often are.

I have applied and shared many of these principles with our team and clients during these unusual times as for many, it has felt like a real struggle to keep going during the pandemic.

**Do more of what gives you energy
and less of what depletes it.
This simple concept allowed me to transform my
energy and my life. Could it do the same for you?**

It certainly worked that way for Jane McDowell, who heads up our Customer Delight Team. Before the pandemic hit, she was about to start a new networking group. But when business dwindled, so did her energy levels. She felt deflated and came to something of a halt. Her thinking was that it would all be over soon (and who could blame her – that's what we were told, and many of us believed it). So, she busied herself with working on her business – ignoring the fact that she had no clients and no work coming in, hoping that they'd be back soon.

Luckily Jane has the HCB community, who were able to show her that the only way she was going to move forward (and perhaps even survive, in business terms) was to take action doing more of what would boost her and her business – and soon.

To do that, she needed to radically change her energy levels and find ways to motivate herself – physically and mentally. She did this by establishing a routine of getting outside and walking as much as she could, and by listening to people and podcasts that inspired her to move forward.

Doing this each day created the energy and focus to completely adapt her way of working, so she could treat clients online and help people from home even during lockdown. Through virtual networking in Bristol, England, she now has clients across the UK and even in the USA – all from raising and re-focussing her energy levels.

**Where in your day or week are you lacking in energy?
What could you do to create and refocus your energy, so that
you can perform to a higher level in your daily life?**

During the pandemic, Anna found it difficult to keep her energy
levels up – in fact she got to the stage where she felt like she'd been
hit by a sledgehammer. Nothing was physically wrong with her, but
she wasn't letting the right energy in.

As we all know only too well, 2020 brought with it a lot of fear, a lot
of negative news stories, and a lot of unhelpful scaremongering. It was
all too easy to let all this in and feel downhearted and exhausted by it.

To help herself move forward and regain her energy levels, Anna had
to consider who or what it was that was stopping her energy. This could
be people, situations or even places. For Anna it was all three – so she
had to find a new routine, one that cut out the news, the people that
weren't helping and the voices in her head that told her she couldn't.
By letting go of all that and allowing herself to be far more present,
she set herself up for daily and future success.

For Anna, creating energy comes from being outside and doing something
physical. Knowing that this is how she performs at her best, she has a
morning routine that incorporates sea swimming no matter the weather
and credits this with keeping her sane through 2020 and beyond.

**How do you raise your energy, what do you focus on?
Who might you need to listen to more, in order to
put you on the right path?**

Amy the Chief Operating Officer at HCB raises her energy by focussing on her goals – which she does by imagining herself having achieved them – what she will see, smell, hear, touch and even taste if she truly succeeds. She gives herself time every morning to experience all those sensations. This 'programmes' her brain to be successful and inspires her throughout her working day, which in turn dramatically increases her energy levels.

As a further daily boost, Amy also does a series of breathing exercises. This helps her centre her focus and get herself in the right mindset for the day ahead along with oxygenating her body and brain. Having breathed properly and focused her brain on achieving success, she starts every working day bursting with energy. She also found that being in the right 'outfit' supported her mindset so getting dressed for work even when working from home was hugely important.

**The discipline of a daily routine
is what creates the freedom of endless energy.**

ACTION POINTS

1. In which areas of your life do you have boundless energy? How come? Who are you with and what are you doing? How can you have more of that in your life?

2. What drains you? Who, what, when, where...? What activities or tasks are you avoiding that you just need to get done? How come? What could you do to get these things off your plate and free up your energy and headspace?

3. What do you need to do more or less of? Recognising that sometimes you must do things you don't enjoy, how could you integrate things you like into things you don't really enjoy, to make them easier or more bearable? What daily disciplines could you implement to create more energy?

CHAPTER 6

A SUPPORTIVE COMMUNITY IS KEY! SURROUND YOURSELF WITH THE RIGHT PEOPLE

*We are the average of the five
people we spend the most time with.*
– Jim Rohn

When it comes to relationships, we are greatly influenced – whether we like it or not – by those closest to us. It affects our way of thinking, our self-esteem and our decisions. Of course, everyone is their own person, but research has shown that we're more affected by our environment than we might think.

Who are the five people you spend the most time with?
**Do they help you move forward or support you growing
into the person or business owner you want to be?**
If they don't, who else might you want to bring into that circle?

While it's ideal to be closely surrounded by positive, supportive people who want you to succeed, it's also necessary to have your critics. You need both positive and negative feedback in order to make progress (though the latter is only helpful if delivered and received in the spirit of moving you forward). This means you need five people around you who love you enough to give you both. Find people who are getting the results you want, spend time with them and do what they do. Learn from their successes and their failures.

This is exactly what Alice did, or rather found herself having to do, as she wasn't surrounded by the right people. But she grew despite them, because she found a supportive community that was willing to help her grow.

Alice started working with us as a client 18 months ago. She had a fledgling copywriting business that wasn't earning very much money at all. In fact, it was barely paying the bills, and Alice will be the first to tell you that she was largely surviving by spending as little money as possible and eating only Cornflakes and rice.

From the first month we started working with her, she consistently earnt at least £1,000 extra a month, right through the pandemic. But it wasn't all sunshine and roses. As her business grew her personal life fell apart, fairly monumentally.

She lost her fiancé, her home and a lot of her friends, as she moved halfway across the country to avoid a destructive relationship. She had considered it to be a fairly normal relationship, but – as happened to so many couples in 2020 – lockdowns brought out its worst and darkest sides. Yet through all this, her business continued to grow – flourish even. Within 3 months she had tripled her income and within a year had built a six-figure business.

How was she able to grow from making next-to-nothing to earning £18k in a single month, despite all the drama going on in the background? By having a supportive community that wanted her to succeed and knew exactly how to help her do it. Her community consistently reminded her of her worth and encouraged her to do more.

Alice's community – the HCB team – also told her what she needed to hear, whenever she needed to hear it, whether she wanted to hear it or not.

Have you got that sort of community around you? One that will lift you up into action when the going gets really tough?

Unfortunately, during the pandemic, many business owners learned first-hand how not every community is the right community. When trying to grow your business and get more clients, just 'getting out there' and networking is not necessarily the answer (although it's a good start). You need to surround yourself with the right people.

David Roylance is an avid networker, and associates with many groups through the course of his working week. These are networks he chose to be a part of, enjoyed attending and got great value both in business and personal terms. But when the pandemic emerged, so did people's fear, scaremongering and negativity.

David would arrive with a positive, can-do attitude and leave drained, demoralised and demotivated. What had happened to his community? The answer is a simple one – they were not bad people, nor a bad group; but they weren't resilient enough to be able to cope when things started to go wrong, or rather, when things didn't go as planned.

People's reactions ranged from conspiracy theories to forecasting doom & gloom and full-on panic. And it appeared to be increasing and extremely contagious.

Your community should lift you up, to support you in both the good times and the bad. With the benefit of a helpful, constructive community on his side in the shape of HCB, David was able to take a step back and take decisive action. Instead of being dragged down by negative mindsets, David created his own business networking groups to replace those that he now chose to not attend. These groups are thriving and doing the job they should for everyone who attends, with David masterfully taking the helm. His supportive community served as the wind at his back, propelling him into action.

If your community knows you well enough, they know when you need catching and when to call you out. Do your communities do that? Could your community support you through a massive life change, even if you felt unsure of yourself?

Would they do it in the middle of a pandemic, when it is so easy to go along with – or even become part of – the 'fear-mongers'.

How did your community react to the pandemic? Who could you spend more time with to fill you with more positive energy and move you forward?

If you can't think of anyone, don't worry – give yourself more time, and perhaps consider expanding your network in a new direction. Perhaps combine this with an activity that lifts you up as well for a double bonus.

What people consider to be a supportive community, is unfortunately usually people who love you so much that they want to keep you stuck – because staying where you are is often safer. But that will not allow you to be all that you can be, and often it's not even comfortable. They want to keep you the same – they're not actively trying to sabotage your plans but haven't evolved enough to realise that you changing is not a threat to them or their survival. Remember, you are not a tree – you can move. You're not stuck where you are, or with the people you currently spend time with.

Regarding the last year in particular, when people have seen others changing, it has magnified their own fear. So, they have (consciously or subconsciously) discouraged the people they love from changing or doing things differently.

Might this be true of some of the people in your world? It doesn't make them bad people. It just means they love you so much that they want to keep you safe. But safe won't move you forwards.

ACTION POINTS

1. Consider your community – who are the people you spend most of your time with? Writing a list may help you gain clarity here – and chances are the results will be fairly illuminating.

2. Are the people on your list willing and able to help you to progress, move forward and be more? Consider each one in turn. How can you augment the influences you have around you in the areas of health/time/work, so that you have more of the positives? This could be through reading books, watching YouTube videos, listening to podcasts. What would tip the balance in your favour? This isn't about ditching the people around you; it's about finding more of what will help you. There is not only one path – there are many options.

3. Think about adding more positive influences into your life. Find – or create – a community that will help you grow and wants that for you.

CHAPTER 7

KNOW YOUR 'WHY' AND CONNECT WITH WHAT YOU REALLY WANT

Nothing can stop a man with the right mental attitude from achieving his goal. But nothing on Earth can help the man with the wrong mental attitude.
– Thomas Jefferson.

Know your 'why'....

Why are you doing this? What's the point? What do you really want?

If you could wave a magic wand, what would you use it for? Who would you help? What changes would you make in your life, or for other people, or in the world in general?

Whatever the answer is, that is your why!

The biggest question with a goal is WHY?
Why is it important? Why do you want to achieve it?
What lengths are you willing to go to?
Have you thought about your why?

There are two different types of people ... and you are one of them. You are either 'towards motivated', or 'away from motivated'. If you don't know what you want, do you know what you don't want?

If you are 'towards motivated', then you are interested in what you are heading towards and what might be possible. Whereas if you are 'away from motivated' then you will be more about what you don't want to happen and how to protect yourself from what might go wrong. There is no right or wrong version of this – it is just the way our brains are wired and neither type is 'better' than the other. We all lean to one direction or the other depending on the circumstance and it can vary in different areas of life or business.

For example, I (Chris) am almost entirely 'towards motivated' in everything. What excites me is always what's possible: the big picture ideas, making things bigger, better or more advanced and generally never even considering what could go wrong. It is one of the reasons I've been so successful and built so many businesses. However, it is also one of the reasons I failed so spectacularly financially many years ago and ended up over £100,000 in debt. I was only focused on improving my skills so I could make a bigger difference with my clients and totally ignored the bits of my business that I didn't like, such as marketing, sales, accounting, along with ignoring the financial implications of doing endless expensive courses that kept being put on credit cards.

Whereas Karene is more balanced between the two and in some areas is strongly 'towards motivated' and other areas is strongly 'away from motivated'. For example, when it comes to finances, Karene is 'away from' and much more focused on damage control and what could go wrong. Whilst I personally find this frustrating at times, such as when

I come up with a new business idea and she points out that it's not going to work financially, it is one of the reasons why she has been so consistently successful financially throughout her life and she has helped us avoid the possible boom and bust scenarios that my tendencies can create because she always focuses on making sure enough money is coming in. In other areas such as coaching our clients, Karene is strongly 'towards motivated' and is entirely focused on what's possible for them and what actions they need to take to make their dreams a reality.

Knowing what motivates you is a very useful insight in understanding what makes you 'tick' and your strengths and weaknesses. If you're not sure which you are, here's some key characteristics of each type: if you are a more 'towards motivated' person, then you are probably super connected with where you are going and what your life will look like in the future. Whereas if you are more away orientated, you probably spend a lot of time analysing and going over the past.

For example, when Anna left teaching, it was not because she was excited about what future she would create, she had no idea what this was at the time – it was because she couldn't face another 15 years of being in a secondary school classroom. In this situation, Anna was strongly 'away from motivated'.

At the other end of the spectrum, when Amy decided to join HCB, she was very focused on all of the lives that she would play a part in supporting and the magnitude of change that was possible for them and her. She was already making a huge difference with her osteopathy and pilates and this new move was a natural extension of that. It is important to remember that even with that excitement and future focus, it was still scary and required change.

When you've worked out your why – what goal might you want to become excited about?

Creating a goal will help you to stay motivated and keep you focused when the going gets really tough. It will also help you to establish when you have achieved great things – and, most importantly, allow you to dream.

What are you focusing on in life and business currently? Where your focus goes, energy flows. So, focus on the good things – the dreams, the aspirations.

Not everyone knows their whys or their goals straight away. That's ok and really quite normal. Just have a go and see where you end up. It's like a muscle and the more you practice this the easier it will become. Play with allowing yourself to think big! Is that little voice in your head already telling you that you're being unrealistic? That you should stay small? Play it safe? Ignore this voice – it is only trying to keep you exactly as you are right now because this is 'safe'. Thank the voice for its concern and allow yourself to dream bigger … even if just for a minute.

If money was no object, where would you be? What difference would you be making? Find your why.

Once you've found yourself a why, set the GPS. If you know where you are heading, everything suddenly makes more sense. That's not to say everything gets easier, but it certainly gets more straightforward.

If you know where you're going, you can start going there. Even if that's just one tiny step. Start small, manageable and messy. Rome wasn't built in a day, and neither will your dreams be – and it won't be easy to get there, not by a long stretch. But you can get there. Believe you can get there and start living it step by step.

Part of having a GPS to steer you in the right direction, is being clear about what you are saying yes to and what you need to say no to. Like a ship coming out of port, if you have a clear course set by your GPS, then regardless of the currents, the waves, the wind and other ships, you can stay on track, even if that means taking a slightly different route occasionally to the one you originally planned. As long as you know where you're going, you can course correct and still arrive at your destination.

Consider these questions...

What or who makes the biggest positive difference to your life?

What could you do right now that would really put a smile on your face?

What do you want MORE of in your life?

What are you most excited about right now?

What are you looking forward to most?

What would you do right now if you knew that you could not fail?

What do you really, really want out of life?

What is your life really about?

What is your purpose?

The answer to these questions forms your dream. And answering the following questions will help organise your goals into tangible thoughts and ultimately help you determine your why.

- Why do you really want this goal?
- What does this goal mean for you?
- What are the benefits of having this goal and how could you make it more specific or measurable?
- Why have you not accomplished this already?
- What are the drawbacks of achieving this?
- Is now the right time for you to make a commitment to achieving these goals?
- What would be the biggest impact from achieving your goal(s)?

Now close your eyes, visualise what it would be like to have achieved this/these goals. Write down what comes to mind. As you write, make sure you're aiming towards something, rather than trying to move away from anything (when setting goals, 'towards motivated' thoughts are more useful as they'll get you moving, whereas 'away from' thoughts will keep you stuck assessing ways to protect yourself).

David Gil Cristobal, our business partner and Business Scaling Officer at HCB, did this exact exercise and found his 'why'. He originally got into personal training because his mother was looking for ways to get moving again after some serious health challenges and he wanted to be able to help her. He had had a successful career as a professional footballer, so he had the necessary knowledge and just needed to focus his expertise to help her. That was his initial motivation, his 'why'.

Over the last 12 months his why has developed almost beyond

recognition (and that's ok, your why can and will change. Just keep resetting your GPS). David owned a string of gyms across Switzerland, which he sold shortly before the first lockdown. This was (he will be the first to admit) not because he had a crystal ball and could see the pandemic coming, but just good timing. And it changed his why.

David remained with the gyms he'd sold on a consultancy basis, and their struggles – similar to those faced by gyms the world over – became his struggles. He found it devastating to watch good, hard-working people's businesses suffer (and in some cases fail altogether), but he also found it incredibly frustrating.

In many cases, what was causing their pain was their own inactivity. They had just stopped – waiting for the pandemic to pass, or they'd decided it was hopeless. Desperate to do something to help businesses hit by the ongoing effects of the pandemic, he partnered with Chris and Karene in a new venture and together they launched a publishing business.

Through this, they help businesses get back into action, market themselves to their target audiences and establish themselves as experts in their field. Having a book helps business owners stand out from their competition. Yet more important, is the training they receive on how to use their book effectively to massively grow their income and their business. David's new business is formed entirely around his why.

What experiences in your life have caused you to change course? Perhaps something happened that forced you to try and help a different group of people? Or maybe your own life experiences mean you could make life easier for people who are going through the same things?

It was her own life experiences that led Jane to change her why and pivot her business, as is often the case for heart-centred business owners. They don't want others to feel the way they have – they want to make life easier for them.

For Jane, this meant forming a unique, drug-free solution to pain management. This came about because she had an adverse reaction to codeine and an ambulance needed to be called. She had a problem – then she had a why.

That incident was a reason to do what she did – she wanted to give people a drug-free way to deal with pain. Subsequently we went into lockdown, and she had to work out how/if she could deliver the same system online. Initially she was resistant to this but has now developed a whole new modality for her business, and a string to her bow that she will use long into the future. She even says that her new way of working can be even more empowering for her clients.

ACTION POINTS

1. Use the questions above to help form your why. You are either towards or away from and can use this knowledge to better define your why in terms that will move you forward. Determine why being more successful is important to you.

2. Create your goals. Be specific. Set the GPS and then work backwards – where will you be in 2 years, 1 year, 6 months, 3 months? This will show you the steps along the way to achieving your goal.

3. Stay connected with your why and your goals. Keep visualising what it would be like to have achieved this/these goals. What do you need to see, hear and think daily that will keep you connected with this outcome?

CHAPTER 8

TURNING YOUR DREAMS INTO REALITY: CREATE A PLAN

People with goals succeed because
they know where they're going.
– Earl Nightingale

When you plan to take action, be precise. Say when exactly you are going to take the action and how many times you are going to do it. But don't be afraid to get it wrong. Start small, start messy – be a progressionist not a perfectionist – and just start.

It's ok to be afraid – feel the fear and do it anyway!

Take the first step – focus on where you're ultimately going and then just begin. Take a step. Make an action. What's the first thing you're going to do? And what will doing that first thing make possible?

If you're still afraid, consider what the worst possible outcome could be. If it went disastrously wrong, how bad would it actually be? Would you survive? Yes, we thought so.

Break the things you plan to do down into small, actionable steps.
That way you can always feel like you are moving forward.

With our clients we suggest that they set a range of goals rather
than a single outcome. We define these as your minimum goal, your
target goal and your mindblower goal. Having a goal range avoids
the extremes of achieving your goal too easily and stopping taking
action too early, vs feeling like your goal is always out of reach,
becoming discouraged and stopping taking action. When you achieve
your minimum goal, you celebrate and reward yourself AND continue
striving for the next level – your target goal. When you achieve this,
you celebrate, reward yourself and continue striving to reach your
mindblower. This way you can enjoy the journey and celebrate the
wins along the way whilst still staying focused on taking action to
make something massive happen long term.

You can use this goal setting method in any area of life or business.
For example, let's say you want to increase your income, which is
the most common goal of people we coach. Perhaps you're currently
earning £1,500 per month and would like to earn £3,000 per month.
This would be your target goal.

You would set a minimum goal to be slightly lower than your target
so it's more immediately achievable and gets you in action, such as
£2,000 per month. Then your mindblower goal needs to be higher
than your target, maybe £5,000 per month. With a mindblower goal,
it should feel a little scary and would blow your mind if you made it
happen, yet it also must feel possible, even if you don't yet know how
you'll be able to do it. In this example, setting a mindblower goal at

£10,000 would be self-defeating as it would be too big a jump from where they are right now and feel unobtainable to anyone struggling to earn more than £1,500.

Using goals this way means you're less likely to fail because it sets you up for consistent success, which means we avoid the classic demotivation that occurs when we fail to achieve something. When you fail you feel bad, and you're far less likely to try again. By consistently succeeding, you will be encouraged to keep going. Try and make your mindblower a bit scary and then take steps to make it happen!

Know the difference between values, vision and goals. Do you know what all three are for you in different areas of your life and business?

Your values are your WHY. Whereas your vision and goals are the HOW you will make that value a reality. Your plan and your actions are the individual steps within the goal describing what you are actually going to do.

For example, if my:

> VALUE is to have a healthy body.
> VISION is to be strong in my core.
> GOAL is to be able hold a 5-minute plank in 3 months.
> PLAN to practice 3 times a week.
> ACTION to increase by 5 seconds each time.

By consistently taking action you will turn action taking into a habit. Your brain is the engine driving you forward, but fear is the handbrake – if you don't let go of fear, you will slow (or even stop) your forward momentum.

Let go of the fear and just do it.
Everything you want is on the other side of fear.

Everything new that you do will make you a beginner, and nobody likes being a beginner. It won't be easy, and you won't be good at it straight away. Accept that and just get started.

This is where Anna, comes in. She, alongside our Coaching Team, helps people build their dream lives on a daily basis. She does this by connecting them with what they really want, but also getting to the root cause of why they haven't taken action thus far and what's stopping them.

She also helps them get unstuck – because the actions they might be currently using are not always the right ones for the changing circumstances – there might be more effective actions to take to achieve their goal. This element to her coaching was brought into particularly sharp focus when the pandemic and subsequent lockdowns happened in 2020.

Around 60% of our mentorship clients were hands-on practitioners at that time, which meant 60% of our clients suddenly couldn't do their job – or so they thought. For many, finding a way forward was a question of thinking outside the box. For some this meant an entirely new way of working, for others it meant supporting their clients in a different way.

That's the advantage of being able to look at a situation from a different, outsider's perspective – this is what Anna is able to bring to her coaching sessions. She doesn't always tell our clients what they want to hear – in fact more often than not, they find what she has to tell them uncomfortable. Instead they get told what they need to know, when they need to know it, which is much more valuable.

A great example of this that Anna encounters time and again is people's blocks surrounding money. We will often hear our clients say that they've sold something, when in fact no money has exchanged hands, they've simply sent an invoice – often without payment terms. Unfortunately, more often than not, this doesn't work, and people change their mind and decide not to proceed, meaning no sale occurs at all.

Fundamentally, most people who are struggling financially dislike talking about money and dread asking for it. This means they actively dislike sales and avoid any discussion that might get to the heart of any genuine fears the client may have around investing in themselves and proceeding with their purchase. This makes the entire experience uncomfortable for both parties and results in neither person getting what they want.

Yet as soon as business owners start working in a heart centred way when it comes to money and sales by implementing win:win systems and simplified payment methods, clients happily pay upfront and the business starts making more money. With this problem solved, money and sales no longer need to be feared and the business owner can go back to simply serving their clients and enjoying what they do.

But when Anna tells clients this, sometimes they feel uncomfortable, resistant and, in some cases, even upset. But these emotions all come from fear, and her job is to tell them what they need to hear, expressed of course with love, not what they want to hear because this is what will move them forward.

Who in your life is honest enough to tell you
what you need to hear, in order to help you move forward?

In 2020 our coaching came into its own – we had to coach our clients to get to where they wanted to be in ways they had never previously considered. But we also had to implement this same way of thinking in our own systems and business as a whole.

As an events business our entire business model was in-person events – whether it was a marketing event to showcase our services to potential clients or a training event where we were supporting and teaching our mentorship clients, our business was entirely based on physically being in rooms with lots of people. Obviously, with the pandemic and multiple lockdowns, our entire business model had to change.

Before the pandemic began, we had only a few employees. By the end of 2020, we had 10 and this continues to grow. In a year when most businesses were struggling and shrinking, we actively expanded, and our company grew more quickly than ever before so we could support our clients better and serve more people.

However, rapid growth and structural changes meant a realignment of roles within the company. It meant sharing responsibilities more, delegating and working together in new teams. Our old way of working had worked brilliantly and allowed us to build a 7-figure business helping thousands of people. But what worked before the pandemic, was not what worked during it. So, Amy, our COO, had to create and implement new systems to make sure everything still ran just as smoothly – if not EVEN better than it did before.

This meant a change for all of us, which – as we know from our own experiences and those of our clients – can be challenging. In this instance, the challenge was Amy's in particular, as she was charged with creating and implementing all these new systems. With a clear goal and our company values at the forefront of her mind, she was able to completely change the way we operated as a company whilst onboarding and upskilling multiple new team members at the same time. Just like our clients, we had to be flexible and find a new way to get to where we wanted to go. We also had to do this one step at a time knowing what the outcome was and taking the next immediate step that would move us all towards that.

Was it always easy?

No.

Did it feel like she was letting go of control?

Yes.

And did it better serve our clients while at the same time setting the business up to grow exponentially over the next few years without Chris or me (Karene) having to be involved?

Absolutely.

For our team and our clients, perhaps the biggest evolution required was how to better support clients' heightened sense of fear and uncertainty. The pandemic has been, and continues to be, a massive source of uncertainty and this provokes anxiety. Some people respond best to this by being supported with tough love such as described above with Anna – a verbal shake-up to get them into action, and simultaneously providing a pillar of support so that they could feel confident in their actions and abilities. For others the support they needed meant someone holding their hand (metaphorically) – not pandering to their worries or scaremongering but being sympathetic to their state of mind and the way their reality had suddenly changed.

Some people react better to being given a push in the right direction, with reminders to keep the end goal in mind, while others need a softer approach. Come to think of it, people are a bit like dogs in that way. I (Karene) know this from our own experiences – we got Goldie (our maltipoo puppy) just before lockdown, which was amazing, as he was (and is) great entertainment and we all love him. He exemplifies this action taking mindset very well, despite being a dog, not a business owner – but the principles are the same.

To house train him we used a lot of positive reinforcement. Every time he did the right thing he got a treat, – this focus on the positive got him to where we wanted him to be a lot quicker than telling him off all the time. He was more motivated to go towards the positive (the treat) than away from the negative (the reprimands). Although, sometimes, he definitely needed to be reminded of the boundaries and what was not allowed. As humans, we tend to be the same.

What motivates you?
What thought patterns move you forwards?
How could you do or think those things more,
to help you move forward quicker?

ACTION POINTS

1. Know what you want. When do you want it and why? If you don't know what you want, spend some time with this chapter and get clearer on what this could be.

2. What's the plan? What's the quickest way to get you in action? Who do you need to speak to now, and what do you need to move you forward? Can you do this right away and how are you going to stay in action?

3. Is there anything that is stopping you? If you're honest about it, is the thing that's stopping you, you? What can you do to change this?

CHAPTER 9

WITHOUT ACTION,
NOTHING CHANGES!

Inaction brings fear and doubt, action brings momentum.
– Napoleon Hill

Wherever focus goes, energy flows.
Embrace the future, don't fear change.
The future is still so much bigger than the past.
– Tim Berners-Lee

This is one of the most powerful life lessons. Those who fear change, even minor change, are often unable to make changes in their lives because they are constantly afraid of failing. Only by taking action, even if it's scary, can you change your future and live your dreams.

The quickest way to do this is to take control of your present and enjoy your achievements. So, make small changes, one at a time, and take back control.

After Sharon's bike accident she lost her energy, her confidence and her zest for life. But she was utterly determined to get it back, so she took back control of her life and did exactly that. She put in place small, consistent actions every day that would move her towards her goal. In her case this meant waking up at 5.30am every day to do exercise. The early start allowed her time to focus on her own needs before the rest of her family was awake and although it was sometimes challenging, she wanted to prove to herself and her family that she could stick to this. She wanted to make a big change in her life and knew the only way to do this was to take small, consistent actions.

Her motivation was an upcoming operation to repair some of the damage done during her accident. She knew that the fitter she was going into it, the better it would go, so she went for it. Did she want to get up so early? No. Did she want to do exercise once she was up? No. It would have been far, far easier to stop, miss a day, give up completely. But she kept her eyes on the prize and totally smashed her goals.

With the help of a personal trainer (remember it is totally ok to ask for help, in fact it is a very good idea), she tracked her progress, so she knew exactly how strong and fast she was when she started, but she could also tangibly see her improvements along the way. This acted to motivate her further and kept her going.

The only thing stopping you, is you.

Sharon proves that taking action doesn't have to be terrifying. Believe it or not it can actually be fun. You may have heard this Thomas Eddison quote before, but it fits in with this concept perfectly: "I never did a day's work in my life. It was all fun."

Karene and I (Chris) are all about bringing the fun into our working lives. We do what we do because we love doing it. To be blunt, we don't need the money. We don't need to work another day in our lives because of the actions we have taken to build a solid foundation, but we do. We work because we absolutely love changing people's lives and allowing them in turn to change the lives of others.

A lack of resources is often blamed for lack of progress: 'I could have succeeded if I had more money / more time / better tools.' Ring any bells?

But these are just excuses. With enough determination, enough flexibility and enough creativity, and taking the right actions in the right order, you can get to exactly where you want to be.

Personally, I (Chris) have found this principle to be true, first to my detriment and then to my success. It could be said that I have something of an 'all or nothing' approach to things. Which used to mean that she would either reap spectacular rewards or spectacularly fail to achieve what I wanted. This was true both in my personal life and my businesses. For example, new hobbies or activities being all-consuming for a few weeks, months or years until they were neglected because I was too 'busy', yet I would long to keep doing them. Or in my Osteopathic clinic where I would work back-to-back 12-hour days for weeks at a time until I would be exhausted and then get sick with a simple bug that would put me in bed for several days in a row.

During lockdown, I found that the same thing was happening with my reading. I love to read and taking time to sit down with a great book is one of life's great pleasures. However, being so busy supporting all of our team and clients during the pandemic, I struggled to make time for reading. The only time I did read was when I felt too tired to do anything and desperately needed to switch off, yet then I would become utterly consumed by a book and would stay up late reading it, to the detriment of my health as well as the other tasks I had on my to-do list.

The thing is, in life, how we do anything is how we do everything.

How I was about reading was actually how I was being about everything. This can create a 'boom and bust' effect on so many things in life, leading to an underlying feeling of instability. Recognising this, I decided to be proactive and start taking smaller, consistent actions, without fail in order to create more stability.

I did this in many areas of my life, ranging from doing daily exercise and a set morning routine in order to create consistency in my health and energy levels, to organising regular team meetings in my businesses so I could provide more consistent support and help team members perform better. With regards to my reading, since taking that decision, I read more than 40 books in 2020. Simple tricks such as reading when visiting the toilet or making sure I read 5 pages before going to sleep, actually taking time at lunch, has allowed me to indulge my passion for reading, whilst still looking after my health and being able to get things done each day.

Such a simple concept and a great reminder of the power of small, regular consistent actions to save us from ourselves.

In order to make this process easier, when it comes to deciding what you should spend your time on, we always say to our clients, do something you really love – and do it for a reason that you feel very strongly about.

> **Do you love what you do?**
> **Do you feel overwhelmingly strongly**
> **about what you're doing it for?**
> **If yes, great! If no, change it!**

Whatever you can do or dream you can, begin it. Boldness has genius, power and magic in it. Begin it now – Goethe

- **What are three actions you could take that would move you forward from where you are right now? (Actions you could take today, or this week)**
- **On a scale of 1 to 10, how excited do you feel about taking these actions?**
- **What would increase that score? (e.g. clearer steps, more support, more fun)**
- **What would 'massive action' look like?**
- **What will happen (or what is the cost) of you NOT doing anything about this?**

Remember, doing the same things but expecting different results is the definition of insanity, according to Albert Einstein, who was a fairly intelligent man.

If you do nothing, nothing will change. You will be exactly where you are now in a year's time, 5 years' time, and 10 years' time. Is that what you want?

Tips for achieving your goals

- Spend some time understanding what you need. This may seem simple but being self-aware is one of the keys to success. Look at all areas of your life … from food and water, to exercise, sleep, laughter, down-time and learning time.

- Appreciate the 80/20 rule (otherwise known as The Pareto Principle): Roughly 80% of consequences come from 20% of the causes – this is true in business and life in general. Identify the 20% and focus your energy there as it will have a far bigger impact than focusing on everything else.

- Learn to play to your strengths. Stop trying to be all things to all people. It is not an admission of failure: it's genius! Work with people whose areas of strengths match your weaknesses – and do what you really love.

- Go for gold … when you're on form! Let's face it, some days we're on fire and could conquer the world … but not every day. Whether you want to call it being 'on fire' or 'on a roll' or whatever, relish and maximise the days when you feel like that and get stuff done! Go back to all the 'things' on your list that you still didn't do (because you really don't want to – or you previously didn't 'feel like it') … and get them done! Plan for success.

- Work regularly on friendships. Cherish and nurture them as your most valuable asset. No person is an island. We need each other and it's often the first thing to slip when we're feeling stressed or under pressure. Acknowledge that and do something about it.

- Remember that it's not the goal that's the most important thing, but rather the journey you go on to work towards it, and who you become on the way.

- And finally (and we would argue most importantly) … If you don't pick up the phone and find out how people are, whether they're your clients, your friends, or your family members, how do you know what actions to take?

ACTION POINTS

1. Identify your best 2 hours of the day. If you are better in the morning, then get stuff done then, if you are better staying up late do it then – do what works for you!

2. What decision have you been putting off which, when you make it, will change your life in some way?

3. List the immediate actions you are about to take. Write them down and then take action on them ... right now, in this moment. Now, tell someone what you're doing and make it real. Now tell 10 people. The more people you tell, the more accountable you will be to delivering what you've said you are going to do!

CHAPTER 10

'BOUNCEBACKABILITY' ...ALSO KNOWN AS RESILIENCE

Every winner has scars.
– Herbert Casson

Ok, so here's the thing ...nothing ever goes exactly to plan.

But that doesn't mean you won't get to where you want to be. It just means you might have to be flexible and resilient enough to find a new way to get there, when things get in your way – which they will – guaranteed!

You will no doubt have heard the sayings, 'you live and you learn' and 'learn from your mistakes', and they're well known for a reason, because both are true.

You do not become successful because everything goes your way and magically falls into place – life isn't like that, much as we all sometimes wish it was. You become successful because when things go wrong, you pick yourself up and start again.

Napoleon Hill, the late great author of 'Think and Grow Rich', told a story about a gold prospector, who was mining a particular area for months and months in the blazing sun, convinced there was gold there. But after a period of time, he became frustrated and gave up, handing over the mine to someone else to prospect. The next person came along and almost instantly struck gold – making his millions. If the gold prospector had only stuck with it a little longer, he'd have got exactly what he wanted. The lesson to learn here is to keep going when the going gets tough because this is exactly when most people give up.

Where in your life or business have you given up and walked away without achieving what you really wanted?
Have you considered that if you had kept doing the right things in the right order you would eventually get to exactly where you needed to be, if you'd only stuck with it?

Don't be distracted by what other people think or say. They are not you and they are not in your shoes. Be confident in the actions you take and believe in them wholeheartedly.

Focus on what's important, and don't let setbacks bring you to a grinding halt. There will be setbacks, it will be difficult, but be resilient – keep going.

Remember that whatever we focus on we tend to attract. So, focus on your goals and why you're doing this. Focus on what's important and don't sweat the small stuff.

We are all a lot stronger than we think we are. It's easy to forget that we have figured things out so far in every area of our lives – all the decisions we've made have got us to where we are now. There is always a process, results may not happen straight away and things may go wrong, or not according to plan. But we can cope. We are resilient - you just have to remember that.

Because just like it did in 2020 and continues to do so in 2021, sometimes life really does suck – but that's ok. There is no joy without pain – having both lets us know that we are alive. Or as Jay Shetty put it: "Life is not linear or a straight line, there will be ups and downs, highs and lows." He also said: "Failures are only failures when we don't learn from them", which is also very true.

Think of this in terms of children (which we all once were, however long ago that may seem). Children (and some adults) have tantrums when they don't get what they want – and also when they get everything that they want. Neither represent the moments of joy. The moments of joy are to be found along the way – when you are getting there and you can see the finish line. Don't forget to stop and take stock.

But remember that everything new takes time to master – tying your shoelaces, learning to walk, catching a ball. The adults in your life, didn't give up on teaching you to walk or read because it was taking too long. Children are great at bouncing back when they don't get things right. As adults we could learn a lot from this.

Over the course of the last year, Anna and her husband decided they wanted to move their family to the countryside. But as anyone who's moved house knows, that massive decision alone is just the tip of the iceberg. The number of ways in which a house purchase can fall through – as Anna discovered – are many and varied.

At one point they decided that the stress and emotion involved in trying to move, alongside dealing with the pandemic and everything else going on, was becoming overwhelming, so they decided to take a month away from the process. To reset, to gain clarity, to rest – and to come back to the task in hand in a better state of mind, refreshed and renewed. They had to bounce back and reset their way of thinking – they had to be resilient. When they returned to the process they refocused and found the house of their dreams and whilst it is still a work in progress, it is certainly closer to their goal.

Whether building a business, having a baby, getting fit or buying a house – in all areas of life – you will encounter challenges, things will not go to plan, you might even 'crash and burn', but you can bounce back. Overcoming any challenges rarely happens instantly. It will take time, patience and sometimes a lot of effort. Bottom line is, it will take action!

Where could you step back and see that things have gone well for you, that you have progressed or moved forwards? Remember how those moments felt because it is important to remind yourself how far you've come and to be proud of your progress.

Let's face it, there are enough reminders in life of what we're not happy with. Spend some time focusing on what you are, and it will help you 'bounce back' and overcome your next series of challenges.

As a team we put this train of thought into action in 2020 a lot! Because – just like everyone to varying degrees – things didn't exactly go to plan for us. The pandemic struck, lockdowns were enforced and our entire business of in-person events came to a halt. We had to find a new way to support all our Mentorship clients despite not being able to leave the house. And we needed to do it in a hurry, because they, like us, were uncertain, shaken and unsure of what to do next.

So, we got online and created a Facebook Live event for our Mentorship community ... every single day. Our clients could listen to our advice, they could ask us anything they wanted, and we could be there live for them every single day to help them through the challenging circumstances.

Is this how we like to work?

Not really because it was really intense and full on!

Is this what we planned to do with our year?

Absolutely not. It was emotionally draining, time consuming and a lot of hard work!

But that's what we chose to do to continue to support them – and it was totally worth it! So many of our clients have had their best financial years ever during the pandemic. And yet many of them work in-person with their clients such as Osteopaths, Physiotherapists, Personal Trainers and Massage Therapists and so had to discover entirely new ways of serving their clients and bringing in revenue. By changing the way we worked, we allowed our clients to see what was possible for them and provided them with continual support and strategies so they could adapt to the situation and set their business up to thrive.

Life will always happen, and the key is to stay flexible to doing things differently so you can continue serving your clients. No matter what happens, focus on what you can do to better serve the people who pay you money. This simple shift in attitude will enable your business to survive and thrive no matter the circumstances.

Remember just because something has always been done a certain way, it doesn't make it right. How else might you be able to achieve the same outcome. Looking more at 'what' you are trying to achieve and then looking at 'how' you might be able to do this will inherently allow you to be more flexible and resilient.

**What do you do when things go wrong?
How do you react if you can't do things the way
you've always done them?
Could there be a more productive way of
coping next time things don't go to plan?**

ACTION POINTS

1. Where is life or business not where you want it to be? Or where have you given up just before it could have been successful? How can you stop that from happening again? Can you recognise that the last step is often the most important one? How can you keep yourself going for a little longer in anything you do?

2. Where in life or business are you reacting in a way that you don't want to? Is it a certain relationship, in a certain set of circumstances or has how you used to feel sometimes crept into how you feel now? Get clear on what life is like. Now make a decision – what do you actually want?

3. Where in your life have you been wildly successful? Identify three times (in any area of your life, not just business), that you have been successful. Remember how those moments felt. Feel that feeling in your whole body – what smells, sounds and even tastes you would associate with that success. Remember that feeling when things aren't going your way. Because you will feel it again.

Now go back through this book, answer the questions, play full out and be curious as to what you might discover. And ... guess what! ... **nothing changes until you actually take action.**

Take the actions you need to move you forward, even if they feel scary. If you don't, you are choosing to stay stuck with exactly what you have right now. Hopefully, by now, we have motivated you to realise there is so much more in life and business waiting for you.

In the words of Dory from the movie Finding Nemo,
"Just keep swimming!"

If you are curious about working with Chris, Karene and the HCB Team to exponentially grow your business and transform your life in the next 12 months, we'd like to offer you a gift of a free Business Strategy Session to work out your best next steps.

To be clear, this session is only for people who are serious about making massive changes to their life, their finances and their business. If this is not you, that's totally fine and we wish you well, and don't waste your time or ours by booking a session.

If you are looking for what could move you forward and help you, perhaps even become one of Chris and Karene's next heart centred millionaires, then register for your free session on the link below and we look forward to working with you!

www.heartcentredbusiness.com/free-strat-call

Would you like to become a heart-centred millionaire?

What if you could exit the day-to-day running of your business and spend more time doing what you actually love?

Whether you're a solo-act or a seven figure company with many employees, there's a step-by-step system that will increase your revenue and free up your time, all whilst improving the results you get for your clients.

How can we be so sure? We created the system - and it has transformed the businesses and lives of thousands of our clients to date.

Now, we're on a mission to create 1,000 heart-centred millionaires.

At Heart Centred Business we typically work with women in their 40's who are running their own business, working all hours and doing everything for not enough profit. We help them to grow their business so it can run with or without them, and they can earn enough money to do whatever they want.

If you're curious about becoming a heart-centred millionaire, book a FREE Business Strategy Session and explore what might be possible for you and your business.

www.heartcentredbusiness.com/free-strat-call

hello@heartcentredbusiness.com
+44 (0)333 987 4245

Did you know that writing a book is the best marketing tool a business owner can have?

And yet, most people either...

- Never write a book because it's 'too hard'

Or...

- Write a book and never make any money from it

What if you could write a bestselling book based on your expertise and use it to grow your business, advance your career and earn a lot of money, all at the same time?

At HCB Publishing we help our clients do exactly that!

√ We help you make money from your book before you write it!

√ We give you a step-by-step writing guide so your book gets written in just 90 days!

√ We edit, proof-read, typeset and publish your book on Amazon so you become a bestselling author!

√ We help you launch your book effectively so it opens doors and creates new opportunities!

√ We teach you how to use your book to actually make money!

As bestselling authors and serial entrepreneurs ourselves,
we know what a huge difference having a book
can make to your business and your career.

If you're curious about writing a book and getting paid before
you even start writing it, schedule a FREE Strategy Session
and explore how becoming an author with HCB Publishing
could change your life.

We're on a mission to create 1,000 millionaires.
Want to be one of them?
Fantastic! Let's talk.

www.hcbpublishing.com
hello@hcbpublishing.com
+44 (0)333 987 4245

Business success powered by great content

Words That Work creates content that gets results

Your business works – you're fantastic at what you do,
your clients are delighted with the service you provide and
you run a team of happy employees …but you've plateaued,
stopped growing, or maybe even ground to a halt.

Why?...

- You're not getting in front of the right people
- When you are in front of the right people, they can't see the value
in what you do
- You're not presenting yourself as an expert in your field

Words That Work can help you with all of this and more.

The power of great content can help you:

√   Be seen by the right people
√   Connect with your ideal target audience
√   Dramatically increase your sales

Words That Work tells your clients exactly what they need to know, in exactly the way it needs to be said in order to get you tangible results, fast.

www.wordsthatwork.uk
hello@wordsthatwork.uk
+44 (0)203 432 7050

Be Seen, Be Heard, Get Paid What You're Worth

What if there was nothing dimming your light?

What if everyone else could see your worth?

What if whenever you talked, people sat up and listened?

- **Women are more likely to do a job that's above them, without being paid for it.**
- **Women are more likely to be dismissed, ignored or disregarded when they speak.**
- **Women are more likely to hear their own words repeated by a man, who will then be congratulated for it.**

A lot of virtue signalling and posturing goes on around equal opportunities, but not a lot of action. Take control of your career path and your life, today.

Speak to Shine is for any woman who:

√ Wants to take charge of the impact they create

√ Wants to provide more value in their role or business

√ Wants to create influence, even when they're not in the room

√ Wants to be the best version of themselves, right now

√ Wants to get paid what they're truly worth

Add £10,000 (or more) to your income every year, whether you own a business or want to achieve more in your corporate role.

www.speaktoshine.co.uk
hello@speaktoshine.co.uk
+44 (0) 203 740 5939

Here's to good health –
the best investment you'll ever make.

Investing in your health is the most effective way to improve your life – which is why it's the best decision you'll ever make.

Because with better health you can improve every area of your life – mindset, productivity and relationships, as well as your physical state. But more importantly, better health can give you more time to do the things you love with the people you love – which we would say is priceless.

BeFueld is the state-of-the-art, innovative supplement from the nutriceutical company of the same name. Formulated to aid recovery and boost your immune system, body and mind, its all-natural energy drinks, pills, powders and meal replacement solutions are all derived from plants and vitamins.

Fuelling active lifestyles

How we fuel our professional and personal lives affects how we feel, function and perform. Many busy people subconsciously choose to fuel their bodies with sugary or caffeinated drinks, which can lead to a dependency that impacts long-term health. BeFueld offers an all-natural, ready-to-drink, healthy alternative.

Fuel your mind

For the resilient entrepreneur, the process of recovery involves much more than muscle repair – it also spans chemical & hormonal balance, nervous system regeneration, and the maintenance of a positive mental state. Whereas the consequences of overworking include: diminished motivation, reduced mental clarity, and ultimately a decline in performance.

BeFueld's vitamin-rich formula facilitates a healthy brain, promotes energy and protects against mental decline. It also enhances serotonin and dopamine production to help you maintain a positive state of mind.

Fuel your body

Exercise without adequate recovery can cause joint & muscle pain, lead to fatigue and weaken your immune system, leaving you more susceptible to injury and illness.

By enhancing the nutrients your body takes in you will aid your recovery and your body will be able to adapt better to any stress you place on it.

**It is not about how much you can endure,
it's about how fast you can recover.
Be fuelled by nutrition and build recovery into every day.**

**www.befueld.com
support@befueld.com**

hcb *Coaching*
Skills and Mindset to transform peoples lives

PART OF THE
hcb *Collection*

**Bored of doing the same old job and want
to do something more interesting?**

**Would you like unlimited earning
otential while you change peoples lives?**

Train with us and become a Coach!

Coaches get paid to help people achieve more from their life,
their work and themselves

Consider, have you ever seen a top athlete or sports person
who doesn't have a Coach?

What about the top entrepreneurs and CEO's?

The top performers in any industry use Coaches to help
them achieve their true potential.

Whatever your life skills or professional experience, we can help you develop world class Coaching skills AND teach you how to build a successful and highly lucrative career as a Coach.

Having built many successful businesses, including a 7-figure Coaching company, we've trained thousands of people how to succeed. With knowledge of what works in real life, rather than just theory, we'll train you how to Coach people for success in any area of life or business and transform your own life and finances along the way.

To register your interest for this upcoming training, email **hello@hcbcoaching.com**

Printed in Great Britain
by Amazon